IT'S NEVER TOO LATE

"A Life Changing Choice"

Patricia Pruett

Women Rich In Faith Ministry
Victoria, TX

All Rights Reserved. Copyright © 2011 Patricia Pruett
No part of this book may be reproduced or transmitted in any form or by any means, graphic, electronic, or mechanical, including, but not limited to, photocopying, recording, taping or by any information storage or retrieval system, without the permission in writing from the author and publisher.

Scripture quotations are taken from the Holy Bible, New Living translation, copyright © 1996, 2004. All rights reserved.

Other scriptures taken from the Holy Bible, New International Version®. NIV®. Copyright © 1973, 1978, 1984 by International Bible Society. All rights reserved.

The names of some individuals have been changed in order to preserve their anonymity. The goal in all cases was to protect people's privacy without damaging the integrity of the story.

Editing and Interior Design by Matt Syverson

For information, please visit: womenrichinfaith.com

Author contact: patriciapruett1@yahoo.com

Women Rich In Faith Ministry
P.O. Box 7637 Victoria TX 77903
(361) 578-2677

Cover Art designed by Jennifer Lane/jlanecreative.com

Author Photo by Divine Images by Erica

Order online from Amazon and Barnes & Noble
Also available for Kindle and Nook
ISBN: 978-0-615-47618-6

Thanks to:

My daughters, Brandi & Sara, who I love with all my heart. You always believed in me and never gave up.

My grandchildren, Landon, Seth, Kaylie, Nathan, & Kenzie Faith – may you know that the generational curse has been broken.

My dear friend, Irma Lopez, for always being there for me.

Joyce Meyer and her television program, 'Enjoying Everyday Life', which I start each day with.

My editor and God-sent dear friend, Matt Syverson, for encouraging me and helping me fulfill God's purpose.

Faith Family Church, Victoria, TX

Celebrate Recovery Program

The ladies of Women Rich In Faith

This book is dedicated to **GOD** for using me to do His work and giving me the understanding that all things are possible through Him.

Trust in the LORD with all your heart and lean not on your own understanding; in all your ways acknowledge Him, and He will direct your paths.

Proverbs 3:5-6

The Serenity Prayer

God, grant me the *Serenity*
To accept the things I cannot change...
Courage to change the things I can,
And *Wisdom* to know the difference.

Living one day at a time,
Enjoying one moment at a time,
Accepting hardship as the pathway to peace.
Taking, as He did, this sinful world as it is,
Not as I would have it.
Trusting that He will make all things right
if I surrender to His will.
That I may be reasonably happy in this life,
And supremely happy with Him forever in the next.

Amen.

Eight Celebrate Recovery Principles

by Pastor Rick Warren

1. Realize I'm not God; I admit that I am powerless to control my tendency to do the wrong thing and my life is unmanageable. *"Happy are those who know they are spiritually poor" Matthew 5:3*

2. Earnestly believe that God exists, that I matter to him, and that he has the power to help me recover. *"Happy are those who mourn, for they shall be comforted" Matthew 5:4*

3. Consciously choose to commit all my life and will to Christ's care and control. *"Happy are the meek" Matthew 5:5*

4. Openly examine and confess my faults to God, to myself, and to someone I trust. *"Happy are the pure in heart" Matthew 5:8*

5. Voluntarily submit to every change God wants to make in my life and humbly ask Him to remove my character defects. *"Happy are those whose greatest desire is to do what God requires" Matthew 5:6*

6. Evaluate all my relationships; Offer forgiveness

to those who have hurt me and make amends for harm I've done to others except when to do so would harm them or others. *"Happy are the merciful" Matthew 5:7 "Happy are the peacemakers" Matthew 5:9*

7. Reserve a daily time with God for self examination, Bible readings and prayer in order to know God and His will for my life and to gain the power to follow His will.

8. Yield myself to God to be used to bring this Good News to others, both by my example and by my words. *"Happy are those who are persecuted because they do what God requires" Matthew 5:10*

PART ONE: *Self-Destruction*

The first memories I can recall start around the age of four. Like most people, I can't remember much before that, but I do know I was taken care of and loved. I have precious few thoughts of my mother and father being together as a married couple. Sadly, the recollections I do have are mostly unpleasant – they deal with anger and fighting and someone getting hurt, either emotionally or physically. Nevertheless, I loved my mother and father and always wanted them to be together.

My parents were very young when they married – my mom was just sixteen years old. As might be expected, the marriage ended in divorce by the time I was five. My mother gathered her possessions and us children and relocated from Port Lavaca, Texas, to Victoria, Texas, to live with my grandparents.

I have two older sisters and one younger sister, so my mother had her hands full. We all moved into my grandparent's house, a home I came to love. It was a large white house, the biggest on the block. It was so big that it easily and comfortably housed two families. My mother and we girls lived upstairs, and my grandparents lived downstairs. I had a secure home, and my sisters and I were all very loved by my mother and my grandparents. They provided us with everything we needed. My mother was very protective and strict, something I didn't much appreciate at the time, but do now. I didn't get to do a lot of the things most of our friends were allowed to do. Although I was very shy, I assimilated to Victoria, and my elementary school years were pleasant.

In spite of many bad episodes with my father, my mother did not keep him from seeing his children. We were able to spend some weekends together, accompanied by other relatives from his side of the family. My daddy was an alcoholic – I always remember him being drunk when I was a little girl. Knowing what I know today about addiction, I realize that, despite his disease, he loved his children very much, regardless of whether he was always there for us.

I was about twelve years old, just about to enter junior high, when my sisters and I stopped getting to spend weekends with my father and his family. My parents just couldn't get along and agreeing on anything was next to impossible for them. As often happens in life, God gave me what I needed when I needed it most. I met a new best friend, Roberta, who still holds that place today.

Things started to change for me, but I wasn't ready. Like most girls entering their teenage years, I was insecure. The boys in school made fun of me because I was very skinny. They called me 'skeleton' and told me I was ugly. Sadly, I believed them. A lot of attention is being given to the problem of bullying nowadays, but back then it was just a part of life you were supposed to deal with or ignore. Not being equipped with the coping skills to overcome this bullying, I thought of myself as ugly from then on. I remember praying to God, asking him to make me pretty.

At that point in my life, I only knew a little about God and Jesus. I was born into a Catholic family – my grandparents were devout. They adhered to the scripture and followed the rules and beliefs they were taught, without question.

Although my mother was raised Catholic, going to church was not a regular activity for us. We never really talked about God or Jesus in our daily life. I did memorize a few prayers, and sometimes we prayed before meals at the holidays, but I didn't read the Bible or know what was in it. I was young – religion was something I saw around me but didn't understand. I saw my grandpa pray on his knees every day in his room, but I was too young to truly understand what he was doing. I knew I wasn't supposed to interrupt him, though, and I sometimes thought he was praying for us girls. It meant something to me, but I couldn't quantify it or have any rational understanding of what he was doing.

My grandpa was a wonderful man. I did

know that. He grew up as an orphan, although he never talked about it. The word 'excuse' was not part of his being, just like others of his generation. He worked as hard as he could each and every day to provide for his family without complaint, no matter how difficult his job was. The main thing I remember about my grandparents is that I never saw them argue. They set an example for my sisters and me, which I thank the Lord for and hope and pray to achieve one day, when God puts a loving relationship with another person in my life again.

Grandpa never talked to me about life or religion – it wasn't in him. He was quiet and didn't express his feelings. He led by example – the patriarch of the family doing the best he could. My grandmother worked very hard, too. She loved to sew and took great pride in the quilts she stitched together from fabric scraps. She also taught my mom to sew. My mother made dresses for us, and we treasured them. They have been passed down to our children and our grandchildren and still hold a special meaning to our family.

Grandma loved her grandchildren so much – the same love I have for my own grandchildren today. I am so thankful I finally understand that beautiful love.

My mother went to college and graduated around this time. By now, she was twenty-five and raising four daughters alone with no child support from my father. She made the right decision, choosing to get an education to provide for her family the best way she could. The journey was difficult, and I admired my mother and loved her so much for the sacrifices she made for her family.

There were times when I didn't care for some of the babysitters mom left us with or some of the boyfriends she chose, but I still loved her and always wanted the best for her. Looking back, I can only imagine how difficult it was raising four children on her own. It's hard enough finding a baby-sitter for one child, much less four.

My older sister, who I looked up to as I was growing up, was the first one that showed me what marijuana looked like. When she was fifteen, she had a boyfriend from school who came over one night when all the adults were gone. We went out in the back yard and smoked our first joint together, along with sharing my first beer. She also informed me that day that many members of our family were marijuana users. If that wasn't enough, she told me we had drug dealers in our family and that my own father had been to prison for drug-related crimes.

I had no clue – I was a naive and impressionable teenager. My first thought was, *Wow, I have a cool family!* I also decided that I now had license to smoke pot and drink beer, since that's what the adults in my family apparently did. I'd had my first joint and my first beer, so I went for broke and smoked my first cigarette that evening, as well.

I hadn't realized it, but a seed had been planted in me that night – a bad seed. It started out innocently enough, but from that point forward it influenced the choices I made. It was now okay, even cool, to smoke pot and drink beer. This is not to say that I became an immediate addict or junkie. In fact, I never repeated the episode until I got to my freshman year in high school. Suffice to say, the apple of temptation had been presented to me, and I willingly had taken my first bite.

I remember the first day of high school. I was so scared about going to such a large school, wondering if anyone would like me. During the first week of classes, I met a lot of different people. I was attracted most to the guys with the long hair, the 'bad boys'. Eventually, all my friends were 'bad boys' and 'bad girls'. My best friend, Roberta, and I hung out with the hippie crowd where we felt comfortable. We felt accepted by them, which means a lot to an awkward teenager.

Eventually, I became a pot head and a cigarette smoker, like the others in my clique. My party life was off and on throughout high school until I got to my senior year, when the switch was flipped to the 'on' position and left there. I was still hanging around with the same kids from school, but there was something new. Older people, 'adults', entered my world of partying. It made sense – the older crowd always had a place where we could party. I am not describing something unique to me – this is the same path countless others have walked.

I tried to keep my drug and alcohol use hidden from my mother, but she eventually found out. I was cut off from hanging around any of my friends, which I obviously did not like. At this point, my relationship with my mother was terrible. Halfway through my junior year, I moved out and went to live with my friend Roberta and her mother.

Roberta's mom let us do whatever we pleased, so that's exactly what we did. She worked two jobs to make ends meet, so she didn't have time to worry about what we were doing. To this day, I consider Roberta's mother, Molly, to be my second mother, in spite of her turning a blind eye to the behavior of the two teenage girls she was providing for.

Finally, my senior year came, and I was elated to be within one year of graduating. I was eighteen years old, and my life was full. I was attending school full-time, plus trying to keep my part-time job at a fast food restaurant, all the while partying as if there was no tomorrow. Little did I know – there very well could have been no tomorrow, the way I was going.

I didn't miss a single party during this period, if I could help it. In addition to the omnipresent alcohol, I started to see different types of drugs at the parties. My life was difficult – it was hell, really, but I thought I was having fun. At the end of the school year, my graduation depended on me passing my final English exam. I have no clue how, but I passed it and was able to graduate with my class. To me, it was just another reason to party.

I didn't have any plans after high school – college was out of the question. At one time I had a dream of attending college, but my mom told me I wasn't going because we couldn't afford it. We never talked about it again.

Immediately after graduating, I became homeless. Still only eighteen years old, there were days I didn't know where I would sleep or if I would eat. My cousin and I would hang out at the bars to find parties to go to, hoping we could find a place to crash. Satan had a hold of my life, and he wasn't going to let go without a fight. He had me where he wanted me, and this was only the beginning.

Six months had passed since graduation,

and I was exhausted from living wherever the party was, sleeping every night in a different place. I decided I needed to get a job – whatever was available. No sooner had I thought the words, it seemed, than I was employed by a traveling magazine sales company, selling door to door.

I was scared to take the job, but felt I had no choice. It actually turned out to be fun. There were about forty of us – all young and traveling around the country and partying together on the weekends. My cousin took the job with me, but she lasted only a month before returning home. Being an adventurous person, I stayed. I enjoyed seeing the country, eating good food, and having a nice bed to sleep in each night.

During the second month of work, the boss man and I became attracted to each other. I loved everything about him, except that he was twenty-eight, and I was eighteen. After a few months, it didn't matter anymore. He and I started seeing each other, and I became his girlfriend. We quickly fell in love. His name was Mike, and he was from Wisconsin. For the first time in my life, I felt loved and wanted, no matter how skinny my legs were. Mike treated me like a queen, taking me places I had never been, wining and dining me. I had everything I had always wanted, and he was the man I hoped to spend the rest of my life with.

Several months went by, and things started

getting a little shaky. I began to hear rumors – that he had other women in his life and was cheating on me. I paid no attention, not wanting to believe that my happiness with my man wasn't genuine. A year went by, and I got pregnant. The first thing that came out of his mouth when I told him was, "You need to get an abortion." It shocked me – I didn't believe in abortions. I love babies. I saw someone very close to me go through one, and it affected her in a horrible way.

I refused to get the abortion, and Mike started to not like me anymore. He said he wasn't ready to have a baby, and he was not going to be a father, either. He didn't want to have anything more to do with me or his child. He said I had chosen my own path, and I would have to live it without him.

My life became very hard. I continued to travel and work for him, but I was miserable. Suddenly, things changed when we traveled to Indiana. I was seven months pregnant. From what I can remember, he and I got into a confrontation, and he left me in a hotel room with all my stuff, saying I was on my own. I cried my eyes out for about two days and had no clue what I was going to do. I knew no one in the entire state, had no money, and had nowhere to go.

I was so scared. I prayed to God for help, and within an hour there was a knock on the door.

Initially, I thought Mike had come back for me, but when I opened the door it was only the hotel's maid. She saw I was in distress and asked me what was wrong. I told her what I was going through, and she felt pity. She took me to her home and gave me a temporary place to stay. She was the angel God sent to rescue me when I prayed for help. I thank God for her every day.

There were no facilities to help me in that part of Indiana, but about a week later I found help in nearby Peoria, Illinois. There was a home there for unwed mothers who wanted to give their babies up for adoption. I had no intention of giving my baby to somebody else, but I needed a place to stay where I could be taken care of. I was seven months pregnant and not under any doctor's care. I remember thinking, *I only have two months left. It won't be so bad.* Those were the longest two months I had ever lived.

On July 19, 1982, Brandi Nicole was born. She was 5.3lbs and 19 inches long. That moment was the first time I had been happy in the last year. I had forgotten there was such a thing as joy until I saw my baby. As my daughter lay on my chest, I said to her, "We are going to get through this, no matter what."

Now I had to figure out what we were going to do. I was all alone when I had Brandi, except for a wonderful nurse at the hospital who held my hand during my labor. She stayed by my side through it all. She knew my situation and understood when I told her I couldn't go back to the home, since I didn't want to give my baby away. She contacted a church that had a woman's shelter. They came and picked us up from the hospital and let Brandi and me stay with them as long as we needed to. I appreciated their help so much, but I was really worried. Now I was not only twenty years old and homeless, but I was a homeless twenty-year-old with a newborn baby.

In my young and inexperienced mind, I believed that when I had the baby Mike would want to come and get us. When I called him, he was on a fishing trip in Canada. It took him two weeks to call me back. He was very cold towards me when we talked. He did not want any details about the birth, but he said he would send me a plane ticket to get home.

One day the ticket back to Texas arrived with a note reminding me once again that I had chosen my own path. I had never been so brokenhearted in my entire life. I was devastated. I was so depressed I couldn't eat, sleep, or think clearly.

When I got home, my mother and step-father, Steve, allowed me to stay with them until I got on my feet. I don't know what I would have done without them.

It's Never Too Late

I was lost. I didn't know much about the responsibility of caring for an infant. I only knew I loved her to death, and I wanted to do the best I could for her. It wasn't long before I got a job and also enrolled in a business college to get some office skills training. I moved into an apartment, so Brandi and I were living alone. I hated it. I was still severely depressed. I found out Brandi's dad had gotten married, and his wife mailed me a letter telling me to leave him alone and that Brandi was not his child.

It felt like my life was falling apart. I was living in poverty and miserable. My relationship with God was zero.

It wasn't long until I started to hang out with the single girls from work, and the bar scene became a big part of my life once again.

I loved the honky-tonk life. Now I was over twenty-one, and a new fellowship embraced me, to the tune of jukeboxes and drunken laughter. I started meeting new people and felt like I had a life again. I looked forward to ladies' night at the bar, since the drinks were free. It wasn't much longer until I started smoking pot regularly. My youngest sister had a friend who sold it, so it was always available.

My younger sister, Millie, and I have always been very close. She helped me raise Brandi during this time period. I don't know what I would have done without her, too.

My drinking started getting out of control, and the more I drank the more depressed I became. I started to fill my need to feel better with not only alcohol, but also with men.

One night, I brought a few friends from the bar home with me. My sister was baby-sitting Brandi for me that evening. When I got home, I brought my daughter into the kitchen to show her off. I asked my friend to hold her while I got a fresh diaper. While I went to the bedroom, she handed Brandi off to another friend. He slipped on some water on the kitchen floor, and Brandi fell to the ground hard.

My daughter was going to die, according to four doctors who told me she would not make it to the next morning. I was so distraught that I made the decision to commit suicide if she passed away. Later that night, with Brandi's blood all over my shirt, I got on my knees and begged God to save my innocent daughter's life. I made promises I really thought I could and would keep. My daughter did not die that night. Today she is a beautiful woman who loves God with all her heart. I stayed sober and avoided the bars for only one month, despite what I had promised God. It wasn't long until I was back to my sinful ways.

It's Never 14 Too Late

The first guy I met when I returned to the drinking scene was the dee-jay at a bar. We started a relationship that lasted about six months, then dated on and off for another year. He wanted to see other girls, which gave me feelings of rejection again.

The next guy I met and became involved with was working on a construction project in town. I started hanging out with him, and it wasn't long until I got pregnant again. I thought my life was really over this time. I knew I was in big trouble. I didn't say anything to anyone until I was about six months along. By then, the project in town was done, and the guy was gone. I didn't even know where he was really from, plus I didn't love him. To me, he was just someone I was hanging out with, getting drunk.

I spent the last months of my pregnancy miserable. I didn't need another baby. I could barely care for the one I already had. I was still hurting from being abandoned by my first love and being dumped by the one guy who had brought me happiness since then, the dee-jay. I was utterly lost, confused and depressed. I considered giving the new baby up for adoption, but I struggled with it. It wasn't until I actually gave birth to her that I knew in my heart she was given to me by God. It was my responsibility to take care of and love my baby. On February 26, 1984, Sara Elizabeth was born. Now I had two babies, and I knew my life needed to change.

About six weeks after Sara was born, I was back in the bars. I met some new people, and we all became friends. One guy was working in Houston and, after hanging out with him for awhile, he asked if I would be interested in moving to Houston to live with him strictly as friends. He suggested I could find a job easily there, and we could be roommates. All I could think of was getting out of Victoria, finding a job, and maybe something good coming out of it. I didn't want to live on a government check anymore, so I packed up my girls and the few possessions we had and moved to the big city of Houston, Texas.

Things went well for several months, until my roommate got into some kind of trouble and was put in jail. It wasn't long before his brothers came for his belongings and said he was vacating the apartment, so I needed to find a place to live by the end of the month.

I had a job working at a brass company doing office work, so I was making a little money. I got a new apartment, which I shared with a girl who had stayed with us a few times at the last place. It was working out well – she worked nights, so I paid her to watch the girls during the day while I worked. We lived together for about two or three months, but one day when I came home from work she was gone. She left me a note saying my girls were with a women a few apartments down. I was upset, obviously, since I had no idea who this women was.

Thank God, my girls were safe. I had no clue what I was to do next. I was ready to give up, but I knew I couldn't do that. I had to take care of my girls.

My life was not going well, once again. I was being sexually harassed by my boss. I felt I had been betrayed by my roommate/baby-sitter. I was living in a rat infested apartment complex in a scary part of Houston – a place where you look out your kitchen window and see police subduing someone to the ground and handcuffing him. On top of all that, I didn't know if I was going to have food to feed my girls the next day, and I didn't know anyone or have any family around to help me.

I had no transportation, which made every movement I made incredibly time consuming and difficult. I was continually borrowing money from work to feed the girls and buy diapers. I was so desperate, I almost married my boss's cousin for money – to bring him into the United States, but that scared me, of course. I was so dumb, I didn't even know it was illegal to do so.

Thankfully, I had applied for a job as office

secretary at a huge scrap metal company in southwest Houston. I got called in for an interview and got the job. It was perfect timing. I was so blessed with this new opportunity at just the right time. Finally, I was actually working for some great people, and I loved my job. I saved up enough money to move into a decent apartment, met some nice people at work who helped me get around town, and was much happier. Plus, my new friends loved my girls.

After I paid all my bills, I would live on the remaining $50 a week to buy diapers for two and food for three. I became a very conservative and frugal person. For the first time out on my own, I was finally finding some peace in my heart. My girls took their rightful place as the center of my life. I loved them so much, and I wanted to be the best mom ever.

My bar scene life ended, and my drinking became not so important anymore. My life stayed balanced for a few months – until I was introduced to the devil drug named cocaine. I met people who worked around me who were doing it, and they started giving it to me for free. At first it was okay, since I didn't know much about it and didn't do much. There was a guy, though, Joey, who liked me and felt sorry for me. He had a business across from where I worked and began giving me drugs and money. He always told me he didn't want me or my girls to struggle, since I reminded him of his daughter.

I had met some neighbors by that point, and I started to share the drugs with them. It was crazy. I found out later that Joey had a bad addiction – he was freebasing the cocaine and smoking it. I was warned by others to be very careful and to never do that. Joey even told me no matter what, to never, ever smoke it. He said it would destroy my life. For years and years that statement scared me, and I made a pact with myself that I would never smoke it. I was twenty-four years old when I made that promise.

As Joey became more and more addicted to cocaine, he and I grew apart. About the same time, I met the man who would later become my first husband. His name was Billy. When I met him, I was tired of being alone. I wanted someone to share my life. After getting to know Billy, I felt he wasn't the right one, but he helped me with the girls and wanted to be with me every day. He loved my daughters and said he would help me raise them as if they were his own. He also liked to have fun. We would go out on dates together, and I felt safe with him. We became very close, but out of the blue he moved to Florida and left me in Houston.

We remained in contact. He said he would come back to Texas if I would marry him. That's exactly what happened, so I married a person I didn't know very well. I just didn't want to be alone anymore. I felt protected when I was with him, and I learned to love him in time. He came from a very dysfunctional family. At the age of thirteen, he was a runaway and lived on the street with prostitutes and drug dealers. He had a lot of street knowledge, obviously, but on the bad side of Houston it made me feel safe that he wasn't afraid of anything.

In our eighth month of marriage, I found out he was selling pot and had sold drugs before I met him. He was also a drug user. He loved to smoke pot, which he did daily. Living with him, I became a pot head again. He also started dealing cocaine, and we became frequent users of that, as well.

I started dealing drugs with him, and for a while I had pretty much everything I wanted. Life was good, but it felt dangerous – we were always moving and looking over our shoulders. We both had full time jobs, and I never had as many friends in my whole life as I did then. We were dope dealers, and dope dealers always have lots of people around. It may seem hard to believe, but I loved my family and still worked hard at being a good mother. It was hard because my daughters saw and heard all that was going on. They witnessed the pot smoking and the drinking in our house. I am sure it became normal to them.

It wasn't long after my third year of being married to Billy that things started to get really out of hand. The drinking and the drugs finally began to bring us down. It seemed like all we did was party – so much that I grew sick of it. I decided I had to get it together and take care of my family the right way. Billy agreed to clean up. He and I had managed to keep our jobs, both of which were great. I still worked at the scrap metal place, and he worked at one of the plants in Houston. Between the two of us, we had a good income, and we did well for a little while.

Billy said he was going to stay clean, but secretly he continued to do what he wanted. Before long, he wasn't coming home immediately after work, or sometimes at all. He was spending all of our money, and we were getting into some serious debt. The lies started, and our marriage began to fall apart. At first I had no idea what was going on. The sad facts were that Billy was free basing cocaine and smoking crack, something I was terrified of. I had seen what it had done to my friend, Joey.

Billy never could explain to me why he did the things he did to me and our family. Finally, one day I saw the truth in what Billy was doing. He was addicted to smoking crack and couldn't stop, even if he wanted to.

He was out of control, which made him very

angry and abusive. I became afraid of him. Within the next year and a half, I left him three times, but always went back, thinking wrongly that he had changed. The truth was, he was only getting worse. Finally, he got into some trouble with the law and was severely beaten by the police – he had broken ribs and a busted-up face, no front teeth.

After about six months of healing, he was back to where he was before that horrible episode. I was hanging on by a thread, struggling to deal with him. I don't know how I did it – I was falling apart, scared for both our lives. I lived in fear everyday, not knowing what was going to happen next. I had no one to help me and couldn't afford to live on my own. Billy ended up quitting his job, so we moved to a tiny, one-bedroom apartment on the south side of Houston.

As if things couldn't get any worse, we lost our car, and I lost my job. Billy and I were doing odd jobs to pay bills. At that time in my life, I knew God was the only answer. I convinced Billy of that fact, and we started seeking churches in the surrounding area and attended here and there. Eventually, I found myself going alone with the girls. We would walk miles to attend a service. After a while it seemed to be too hard, and we stopped attending.

One day a man Billy was working for invited us to a new church, and we went. I remember walking in – the congregation was singing with their hands in the air and everybody seemed so happy. For the first time in my life, I felt the earthly presence of the Lord. The church was called Lakewood Church. I loved it, but for some reason we never went back.

Things only got worse at home. I woke up a couple of nights with Billy trying to slip my wedding band off my finger. He wanted to trade it for crack – he was that desperate and addicted.

Eventually, another ring *did* disappear, but I just thought I had misplaced it. It was precious to me, because my mother had given it to me when I turned fifteen. One day, I was walking to the laundry room and saw the neighborhood crack dealer. My treasured ring was hanging on a gold chain around her neck. My heart sank, but I was too scared to say anything.

I was finally at the end of my rope, but I didn't know what to do. I ran home, walked in, and saw Billy holding his crack pipe. I remember saying, "Let me have that. I just need to know what it is that makes you do the things you do." The choice I made at that moment changed the rest of my life. Living with Billy from that day became a wide-awake nightmare.

For the next six months, I became a full-blown drug addict. I was now twenty-eight years old with a husband who couldn't help himself, much less me. I had two young daughters who had virtually no mother. We were all in trouble, and I had no clue how to right my life. I was out of control. I would wake up and say to myself, "I am not getting high today," but by the end of the day, I had always broken that promise.

I lost so much weight – I was down to about eighty-five pounds. I was stuck, with no money to move away or change my family's circumstance. We were scraping by, begging for food and stealing from grocery stores to feed the girls. Luckily, Billy was getting unemployment checks that paid the rent and kept us from living on the streets. To get out of this financial tsunami, we went back to turning some serious dope. We didn't make any money, though – we just supported both our habits and became even more addicted. How he and I didn't end up in prison or have my girls taken by Child Protective Services is a miracle.

It may have been paranoia from the cocaine, but I always felt like Billy and I were being watched. I knew what I was doing was so wrong and really wanted out, but I could not escape the mess we had created. It finally came to a dire conclusion – we became homeless and lost just about everything we had.

We stayed with a friend, where we had no choice but to stay sober. We both found jobs and saved up to get our own place. Within two months, we were both getting high again. It was time to make a serious change or suffer an even worse fate than becoming homeless again. I called my sister and packed up my girls and moved back to Victoria. Billy had nowhere to go, so he stayed in Houston for a bit, but eventually followed me.

I took him back, and we started our lives in Victoria with a different approach – one that we thought was right. We stayed away from the cocaine, but we still drank and smoked pot. Everyone we were around smoked pot, so we thought it was okay.

I was convinced I could never live a completely sober life. I thought it was impossible. When I think about it now, it *was* impossible for me *then*, because I did not know God like I know him today. Our lives in Victoria became structured – I had family to watch over us. We both found jobs, and our life seemed normal for a change, but things still weren't right. The verbal abuse and pushing around was still there. No matter how hard I tried, I was not happy with him. I hated the way he treated me and my girls. At times it felt like we were his slaves.

A few years went by, and we continued to live in the same manner – drinking, smoking pot, and not respecting each other. I was close to hating Billy. I was very co-dependent, though, and

I couldn't afford to live on my own, so I stayed with him.

One day, my sister, Millie, was invited to a church with a co-worker, and she invited me to go with her. The church was located by the airport and was called 'Faith Family Church'. I had heard advertisements about this church, and they had always caught my attention when they said it was 'a church with a heart'. I liked that.

The first time I went, I was so excited to possibly find a place of worship in Victoria. Millie and I took our daughters and had a wonderful time. Millie and I even got saved! I'll never forget my salvation partner, Anna Query. She is still one of the wonderful friends in my life to this day. I loved the church and wanted to be a part of it. I continued to attend regularly, and my husband eventually attended and was saved, too. He and I even got involved in the recovery class they had upstairs. I remember when we first attended – I would pray that no one would see us go up the stairs.

We kept going to church and started reading the Bible, something we had never done before. I remember nights when we would think about using, but instead we would sit together and pray and consult the Bible. We had so much to learn, but we were trying. We also started connecting with some of the people we met at the church.

Millie ended up moving to Tennessee, and my mom and my stepfather moved into her house. Billy and I and the girls moved into my mother's old house. I started to see great changes taking place in my family.

I was so excited! Things seemed to be getting better – until Satan came knocking on the door once again. Within a rocky two month stretch, my relationship with Billy completely fell apart. He moved to Florida on the day before Thanksgiving in 1995, and I have never seen him since. That door was closed once and for all, never to be reopened. Ten long years with him, and it was over, just like that. Satan had destroyed the happiness Billy and I had for that short time since we moved to Victoria and made our future together impossible.

At the time, I thought it was for the best. I believed that all my problems and anything that could harm me were gone forever, as if Billy had taken Satan to Florida with him. I found out real quick that the devil doesn't go on vacation. He still had his eye on me. He was going to try to destroy my life.

I thank God every day for putting my home church, Faith Family, in my life when he did. In spite of all my struggles and the mistakes I had made, I knew I could reach out to my church family, no matter what. I didn't know it, but I had a ton of work ahead of me, and it was going to be the beginning of a new life with God that I could never have imagined.

A storm was coming my way first....

It's Never 28 Too Late

PART TWO: *The Road To Recovery*

Now Billy was gone, but I still had my job and my daughters. We still had a roof over our heads, but only enough food to last a week. I had no clue how I was going to do it alone, but I knew I had to.

My job was going well. I met a girl who was looking for a place to live, so I invited her and her two girls to stay with me. It would help both of us financially. We all got along great, but we were both single, so off to the bars and parties we went. It was the usual routine. The drinking started first, followed by the drugs. I was hanging around pot smokers and cocaine users once again. In my mind, I thought we were safe, because we never spent any money on drugs.

I felt so much freedom. I could do whatever I wanted, and it didn't seem to have any negative consequences, since other people were paying for my party.

I allowed Brandi and Sara to spend time with their friends and gave them freedom to go places, which they were never allowed to do before. I was letting them make their own decisions, so I could concentrate on what I was doing.

Three months later, in January of 1996, I

met the man I thought I would spend the rest of my life with. His name was Keith, and he was incredibly kind and nice. Being with him made me feel genuinely loved and respected. Looking back, I realize that I was co-dependent and always needed someone to be in a relationship with, whether it was truly the right thing to do or not. I should have spent more time on my own and worked on myself after breaking up with Billy, but I jumped into a rebound relationship.

Being with Keith was much different than being with Billy. He treated me with respect, something a man had never given me. He took me out on nice dates and introduced me to some good people. Keith and I grew close and moved in together after only three quick months of dating. He was so easy to fall in love with. I was trying hard to stay away from hard drugs, but we did drink together and smoked pot.

Six months later, we bought a house together and officially became a family, even though we weren't married. Keith treated my daughters as if they were his own children. I loved him and he loved me and we were all happy together. Keith and I drank on the weekends, but since I didn't party every day, I thought I was okay. I was still sick in my addiction, though, without even knowing it. This relationship meant everything to me, and I was willing to do whatever it took to make it work. When Keith was injured at work, I took good care of him – I didn't want him to suffer. He had broken his femur and was bedridden for a time. I had to take charge of the move into our new house.

Four years into our relationship, Keith finally married me. I have to say it was one of the happiest moments in my life. I had every intention for it to be forever, through sickness and health, for richer or poorer.

The first two years of our marriage were blessed. We got along very well, both worked, saved money, and lived comfortably. I spent some money on cocaine behind Keith's back, but it wasn't a lot. I felt like I had control of my addiction.

The second year we were blessed with our first grandbaby, Landon, born to Sara. Keith and I helped raised our precious Landon as if he was our very own. The love I had for that child was so amazing – it could have only come from God. I was still struggling, though. I was able to give up the pot smoking when Landon came home from the hospital, but I couldn't give up the cocaine. As time when on, I continued to use, increasing in frequency and amount until my life started to become unmanageable. I knew I had to do something to change my circumstance, but I didn't know where to start. My life was in trouble and so was my marriage. I hadn't given up, though – I wanted to save them both.

I took my first step in November 2003, when I walked into Celebrate Recovery at Faith Family Church. It was very difficult, but thank God I did, because I met Pastor Leonard Johnson, the leader of the program. He ended up guiding me through my recovery, along with a wonderful lady who encouraged me, named Irma Lopez.

For the first time in my adult life, I was living in sobriety. I faithfully started attending church, and Celebrate Recovery became the most important part of my life and the highlight of every week.

Anna Query, my salvation partner from 1991, was still attending Faith Family, and we were reunited. She recommended I read a book called, 'The Purpose Driven Life'. She told me the book would change my life, and it did. It was amazing to see how much my life changed over the course of only forty days. I became very hungry for the Word and within ten months I had read the Bible from front to back. I was becoming more a part of my church community, connecting with people and trying to be of service.

I started to see many positive changes in my life, and my family was very proud of me. My marriage became healthy again and so did my relationship with my two daughters. Now I also had a new grandson, Seth, who was born in 2003 to Brandi.

It was an awesome feeling to start the year of 2004 restored. My daughter Brandi and her boyfriend and Seth were now living in Florida. Sara and her boyfriend were living on their own. Keith and I were doing well, very happy, just the two of us. We became even closer and spent a lot more time together. Keith would also occasionally attend church with me, which made me proud and happy.

In May, I had some tests run and had to be admitted into the hospital to have surgery. I was also diagnosed with the hepatitis C virus, which I will talk more about later. My surgery became a nightmare, and I had some serious complications. As a result, what was supposed to be a two day stay in the hospital lasted over a month. I was very ill and ended up having three different surgeries. My life was in imminent danger – I even spent several days in the intensive care unit. I felt Satan trying to take my life – he didn't want me to serve the Lord. He was out to get me, more so than ever before. I experienced so much pain during my stay, but I prayed and read my Bible to give me strength. I always believed that God was going to get me through this, and he did. God had performed yet another miracle in my life.

During my stay in the hospital, I was heavily medicated for pain, but I remember people from the church coming to visit and praying for me. Irma Lopez took food to my family at home, which was a blessing.

I was healthier upon being released from the hospital, but now I had to battle and conquer the hepatitis C virus. I was very afraid, because I had read and heard many bad things about the treatments. I knew I had to take care of it, though, or I would die.

Brandi had come home to be with me through my stay in the hospital. She saw the torture I had been through, so she invited me to beautiful Destin, Florida, for a two-week vacation to recuperate before I started the course of treatment for the hepatitis. It sounded great to me, so off to Florida I went. We had a great time, and I got to see Seth take his first steps, which I will never forget.

Toward the end of the trip, I started thinking of Keith more and more. I missed him so much. When I got home, he was so proud to show me the dishwasher he had installed for me while I was gone. It meant so much to me – I had wanted one for years. The memories I have of that moment make me laugh and cry at the same time, and I will never forget. Thank you, Keith.

It was now July, and I was almost fully recovered from my surgeries. It was time to start preparing for the difficult treatment for my hepatitis. I found a wonderful doctor who was going to help me through it. I felt ready, because I knew I was sober. I was serving the Lord and had faith he would carry me through this trying experience. I also knew Satan was out to kill, steal, and destroy me, through any means.

After further tests, it was determined that the count of the virus was very low, so I was only required to take a six month treatment, after which they would do more tests and determine the future course of action. The doctor scheduled my treatment battery to start in October. This gave me a few months to prepare – I had to make arrangements with my job that would allow me to work when I could, since I still had bills to pay during the treatments.

A sad but amazing coincidence occurred at this time. My pastor at Faith Family, Jim Graff, was also diagnosed with the disease and would be taking the same treatments during the same time frame. I remember feeling so sad for him, more than I did for myself. I didn't think he deserved to have to go through the excruciating process, but I knew he was a strong man with the faith to carry him through with God's help.

As the treatments neared, I felt more and

more afraid. I knew I was going to have to inject a needle into my stomach, something I thought I could never do. I could feel Satan breathing over my shoulder, trying to defeat me. The month of August came around and brought with it bad spirits and low self-esteem. My recovery took a backseat to worries and fear. I was hopeless and helpless, drowning in self-pity. I was on my tenth month of sobriety, but I wasn't taking an active part in it. I was weak, and the devil knew it.

Satan swooped in and stole my sobriety in a matter of seconds. I had been invited to a friend's birthday party – a friend who I had consciously been staying away from since I had become sober. I knew there would be alcohol and drugs there, but I went anyway. Before the party ended, I had a beer in my hand, a cigarette in my mouth, and a line of coke up my nose. I didn't even make it home until the next day. I had lost the battle – I was weak. I had humiliated myself and my family. I can't put into words the failure I felt at that time.

I had relapsed, but only my family and I knew about it. I promised them I would stay clean, but my life became a total lie, meant to fool everyone, even me. I continued to attend church and the Celebrate Recovery program, because I was due to start my treatment and full of fear. Fear is the weakness that allows the chink in your spiritual armor to be exposed – the small crack that can be your fatal flaw. Satan, in all his evil power, saw my Achilles weakness and once again entered my mind through it.

I knew I desperately needed sobriety at this time, but I was so full of guilt that I couldn't stop beating myself up over my relapse. I could not accept that God forgave me for my indiscretions, even when I couldn't forgive myself. My lack of understanding that my God was a forgiving God who wanted me to be happy and free from guilt let Satan have his evil influence on me.

October came quickly, and I convinced myself that starting the treatments was going to keep me from using. I knew I couldn't be abusing cocaine if I was taking such a powerful drug to treat my hepatitis. My daughter, Brandi, moved back home from Florida, which I hoped would be another reason to stay clean. I could feel Satan laughing at me. He knew I was still weak in my faith. I wanted all these other things to keep me clean and sober, but that's not how it works. The only one who can ultimately keep you sober is you, with God's help and that of other sober people, of course.

My treatments started, and I was terrified. My family and I did some intensive research on hepatitis, and what we learned was scary. The treatment had many side effects, such as fatigue, headaches, flu-like symptoms, loss of appetite, depression, low levels of red and white blood cells, and hair loss. My family was understandably concerned, but very supportive. Everyone, including myself, thought all the effects of the hepatitis medication would keep me from using cocaine. None of us understood the power of narcotic addiction, though.

I started the treatment with one injection of interferon and six ribavirin pills a week. At first I had to have help injecting myself. I wouldn't do it without my husband and my daughter standing over me.

A month went by, and I had my first check up. The doctor found no trace of hepatitis in me. I knew I had been healed, since I had never lost faith in God. The doctor decided I must continue treatments for five more months, though, since hepatitis can go into remission and then reappear worse than before.

During the first month of the treatment, I lost twenty pounds and had no appetite. I struggled at work, always feeling tired and weak, but I continued to do my best, since I had the responsibility of managing a retail store along with the obligations of my family. My red and white blood cell counts became very low. I was coping well, until I started to lose my hair. Then I became severely depressed. I was a mess and very sick, and it seemed like the world was crumbling around me.

My doctor was concerned and sympathetic, so he altered my treatment. He prescribed another injection called erythropoietin to help level my blood cells. He also added a medication for my appetite, called Marinol. Marinol is a man-made synthetic form of the active ingredient in marijuana. One thing most people know about marijuana is that it makes you hungry, 'the munchies'. That's why Marinol is prescribed for the loss of appetite.

The doctor couldn't give me anything to stop the hair loss, but he did give me a prescription for an anti-depressant. Nevertheless, I still cried every day. My life was so unmanageable, and I was so powerless. I was hating life.

At this point, I was injecting myself twice a week and taking ten pills daily. The good thing was that, for the first three months, I had managed to stay sober, but that was only because I was scared of possible side-effects with the medication I was taking.

By the end of the third month, my treatments seemed almost normal and expecting the refrigerated Fed-Ex package containing my injection was part of my routine. I can still hear my daughters say, "Mom, your meds are here, I put them in the refrigerator for you." I always looked forward to the appointment with my doctor, hoping he would say I could stop, but he was determined to keep me on the treatment for the entire six months.

I made it through the holidays, and the new year began. I was still clean, as far as drugs and alcohol. If I could just make it until the end of March, I would be done with the treatment. At this time I really believed I was safe, that the choice not to use was being made for me because of my treatments. I was still living in denial about ever having an addiction.

But my will still wasn't God's will, no matter how much I thought it was. I found that out very quickly when I drove by an old drug user acquaintance's house and made the choice to stop in to say hello. To make a long story short, I didn't walk out of that house until two days later. It was a miracle I even walked out at all. If you have ever made bad choices about drugs, you may know the feeling I'm talking about.

This episode made me know I was a full blown addict, and that Satan was going to kill me if I didn't change my ways. I had so much shame, and my family was very disappointed. I wanted to die that day, rather than face my family. I loved my husband and my family with all my heart, but not one of them understood me, and I didn't expect them to. I made some really bad choices, nothing to be proud of. Satan had full control of my life, and I still didn't know it. My life was completely upside down, but I was not ready to admit I was an addict. My pride and my shame kept me in denial.

I was taking the treatments, going to the Celebrate Recovery services, going to church, but still killing myself slowly by drinking and drugging. I was living a double life. I was mentally tormented. My mind was struggling to deal with the rigors of the hepatitis treatment and also trying to convince myself that I didn't have a problem. I had not been restored to sanity, for I was not the person God wanted me to be.

During the day, I worked hard and took care of my family, but many nights I walked with Satan. I almost had a split personality. The good part of my mind so desperately wanted to do the right things. I wanted to get better and be a wonderful employee, a loving mother and wife. I also wanted to help others in their recovery and listen to God and be obedient. I wanted to be more active in my church. It sounds crazy, but I even wanted to lead a group for women in recovery.

I wanted to do all these things and help people, but I needed to help myself first. I was focusing outward, rather than inward. Grandiose dreams, such as those I just mentioned, would soon be answered by evil thoughts that made me believe I was worthless – that I would never change or ever be a good mother and wife. I knew I would never be accepted at my church because of my past. I would always be known as a drug addict and a liar and never be able to hear God and help others. I *was* capable of doing all those good things I wanted to do, but I kept hearing Satan tell me I couldn't. The sad part – I believed every word he whispered in my ear.

I finally reached the sixth month of treatment, and it was time to stop all medications. The day I went to my last doctor visit to be released from treatment, I disappeared for two days, doing nothing but drinking and using. I remember that last night of miserable intoxication. I wanted to die, but I didn't have the guts to kill myself. My soul already felt dead.

The next morning I picked up the phone and called my job and quit, a decision made without asking God if it was right. I irrationally decided to move to Corpus Christi and start a new life. I didn't realize it, but I was running away from my problems, rather than facing them. I informed my husband that I had to leave and packed my stuff, cashed out my 401K, and left. I did not pray about it one time. Not long after moving away from Victoria, I realized I had lost my mind, lost my home, and lost my husband, all in one fell swoop. I had made a huge mistake, but it was too late to go back and fix it.

I did realize I had to seek God for help, for He was the only one who could help me. I immediately found a church. I knew I needed to get connected with some type of recovery program, but my mind was so confused with doubt that I found myself in a severe depression. I was lost in myself, self-absorbed and wallowing in self-pity.

I started praying and reading my Bible and asking God to restore my marriage. I was so focused on getting my husband back that I started to believe I had overcome my struggle with my hang-ups. My attention had simply been redirected for the time being, away from my internal problems. My husband took me back, and we tried to work it out, but four months later he left me for good. It took another fifteen months for him to finally divorce me. A few months after it was finalized, he remarried.

Living by myself, drowning in shame, guilt, regret, and pity, was the most painful thing I ever had to do. During all this mental anguish, I went back to work in Victoria and was right back where I had left off. I felt truly alone and didn't care if I lived or died. My two daughters feared I would kill myself. Satan had absolute control of my life, and he was out to do me in this time. I was in such a bad way that I overdosed and spent Christmas day in the hospital in the intensive care unit, but that didn't even stop me. The constant nights of overindulgence and threats to my freedom if I got caught couldn't stop me, either. It seemed that nothing would.

Then the day finally came – the day that every recovering addict thinks of to keep them sober. I walked into my daughter's house and saw my children, Brandi and Sara. For the first time, I felt the hurt in their eyes and the worry in their souls. I saw all the pain that my addictions had caused them. They had never given up on me and were always there to take care of me when I didn't care if I lived or died. I saw my two beautiful girls, tears in their eyes, and thought of the grandchildren that I bought gifts for to make up for my absences. I was overwhelmed, overcome by emotion and finally willing to change.

I cried so hard that day, because I saw myself for the first time – a woman who was depressed and wounded, a woman who hated herself, a woman who was selfish and inconsiderate. I finally realized I needed help. I had to face my giants and slay them like David did Goliath. I knew I had to get away from the people, places, and things that were tempting me and go to a place where I could build a new, real, personal relationship with God. I wanted to be happy and at peace and know serenity.

I prayed about it for hours, then packed my bags to go to rehab, a place I said I would never go.

It's Never 44 Too Late

For once I was running toward help, instead of running to escape. I wanted to get better so bad that the pride and the denial I had carried for almost all my life completely faded away, and nothing else mattered, except getting right with God.

So off I went with my Bible, and I was not coming home until I was a changed woman. I knew God was going to walk with me through this difficult process. It took sixty days of rehabilitation, but I walked out the door after it knowing I would serve God for the rest of my life. I would fulfill the purpose God had set out for me from the beginning. God had showed me a vision, and I knew it was to prepare me to do his work from that point forward.

PART THREE: *Is It Too Late?*

In the black tunnel of self-doubt and self-pity, many people think of giving up. They feel worthless and unable to change. Some even come to the rash conclusion that life isn't worth living – that it is too late for redemption.

It is never too late! Anything is possible and anything can be overcome, if taken one day at a time. So many others have done it this way, then dedicate themselves to helping others recover, and you can, too. The first time I was told, "Take it one day at a time, that's all," I didn't understand. I didn't want to do it that way. I didn't know that hundreds of thousands of people had bettered their lives with this simple philosophy.

I was stubborn and resistant, like many are when starting the process of recovery. I didn't want to be simply categorized as an 'addict' and told to do what the other recovering addicts did. I thought I was special. In truth, we are all special as individuals, but we are also very similar. I needed to let go of my ego and learn from the actions of others who had walked the same path before me.

I was terrified at first, because I remembered those days in the recent past when I had fallen and couldn't bounce back like nothing had happened. I didn't trust myself to avoid temptation and do the right thing, always.

I didn't know why I felt like this at the time, but now I do – I didn't place my trust in God. I needed to let Him make my decisions for me, but I didn't have enough faith.

In 'The Life Recovery Bible' in **Job 28:28** it says, *"The fear of the Lord is true wisdom, to forsake evil is real understanding."* When we begin to understand the truths from the Bible, we can start to trust God and have hope and faith in the path He has chosen for us. He will give us the strength to make the right choices, if we let Him be our guide – one choice at a time, one day at a time.

So, with my understanding of God's will for me, I realized 'one day at a time' was the only way to have a successful restoration. The Bible says, *"So don't worry about tomorrow, for tomorrow will bring its own worries. Today's trouble is enough for today."* **Matthew 6:34**.

Think about the meaning of that verse! It is so powerful. It says to only think about today, which to the person in recovery means 'one day at a time'. Do the right thing just for today, then get up tomorrow and do it again. Turn it over to God, for without faith in Him, all you will have is worry. Put things in God's hands and try not to agonize over possibilities and outcomes you cannot control. Say the Serenity Prayer when worry consumes your mind. You will feel at ease.

It's Never 47 Too Late

When living in the world without God, I encountered many women in their addiction. They ranged from the age of eighteen to some over sixty years old. Some of the younger women still had hope to get out of their sinful nature, but the women from the age of thirty-five up seemed to feel that it was too late to change. Their hearts were filled with hurt, shame, denial, and Satan. Their dreams had been shattered. They felt lonely and unloved. Some had been abandoned by their families with no hope of reconciliation. Some had lost their children because of their addictions, causing them to anesthetize themselves in their pain, turning to more drugs and more alcohol, not having the strength or the means to cope.

I identified with them now, seeing myself for the first time as being similar, rather than different. Most of these women didn't know there was a God that could save them, just as I was once blind to that fact. I didn't immediately realize how much I could help women like this. At first, recovery is all about *you*, but it becomes much more than that over time – it is important that you be of service and help other addicts in their recovery. Finding a sponsor or accountability partner who will help counsel you is very important early in sobriety. At some point, you will be ready to sponsor others.

This part of recovery is a major transition. It

is a time when you become less self-absorbed and realize that helping others fight addiction is very important to your own long-term sobriety. Early in recovery, it is easy to focus so much on yourself that you ignore others you can help. Imagine that you are in a lifeboat after the Titanic went down. So many are crying out for help all around you. God has blessed you with a life raft. That could be you out there drowning in the icy darkness. What should you do? The answer is obvious – you need to help as many people as you can.

When I was early in recovery, I thought these other women were different from me. I know I've mentioned that numerous times, but it's very important. I felt they were not like me – I was special, an individual, with talents and problems unlike anyone else. Later, when I could honestly look at myself and take a true personal inventory, I realized all these addicted women had many things in common with me. I started to see how similar we all were and thought less and less about how different I was. The fact is – if you find yourself in an A.A. or Celebrate Recovery meeting, you have a lot in common with those around you.

I often think back to the stormy circumstances of life during my addictions. I was like a boat being tossed about by angry waves in the middle of some unknown black ocean. Sometimes my boat was little – when I was depressed and beaten down by the consequences of my actions. Other times my boat was enormous, like the Titanic – when my ego told me I was in control. I didn't need God because my big boat could not be sunk.

But – when my unsinkable ship hit the iceberg, I had no lifeboat. I only had what so many other damaged women have – hurt, shame, denial, and Satan.

During this time, I wondered what my life would have been like if I would have taken the time to learn the truth when I first gave my life to Christ, many years before I got clean and sober. It is easy to fall into shame and guilt when analyzing your past. You have to realize that God has planned everything that has happened to all of us. We no longer need to wallow in guilt about the past if we truly want forgiveness. The things that have happened are the things that have led us to the place we are at now.

It took time for me to understand that, though. Nothing in recovery happens overnight, especially the things you want the most. A new job, a new relationship, a new life – these things take commitment and patience to obtain. I spent almost two years of my life punishing myself, because I had no understanding of why I had done the things I did. I had hurt people I loved with all my heart, and I didn't know why. I had no control, and I couldn't change the past, but I was doing the right things. Slowly, God was working in me. Most miracles don't come like the parting of the Red Sea. They take time.

Patience is not a virtue most modern people have. We live in a society obsessed with instantaneous gratification. Recovery cannot be ordered in the drive-thru lane. It takes real effort. God is there for all of us, but we have to do the ground work.

John 10:10 says, *"The thief's purpose is to steal and kill and destroy."* This is another Bible verse that deserves analysis. Sometimes it can be hard to understand the Bible, since we speak very differently than the way it was written. One way to get to the root meaning of Bible verses is to look at the key words. The key words in this passage are: **thief**, **steal**, **kill**, **destroy**. Who do these words best describe? Here's a hint – his name starts with an 'S' and ends with an 'N'.

The devil definitely broke into me, like a ***thief***. He ***stole*** my relationships with my family. He was in the process of ***killing*** me, when I starting screaming and praying with all my heart for God to please help me. The devil did not ***destroy*** me, though, because God was there for me! If I had not reached out at that time, I would not be alive today.

I was so close to death at that time of my life. I often imagined my body being found overdosed or murdered, left in a ditch beside some desolate road. I did not want to die in such a devastating way! The love I had for my family couldn't end like that. I knew I had to change before one of those ugly visions came true. I was finally determined to do whatever it took to overcome my addictions. I knew the devil had a hold of me, and I was scared, but until one truly understands, one can never overcome.

I was terrified that it was too late to change my ways. I was stuck in my addictive behaviors. These bad behaviors had become habits – *bad* habits that would be so hard to change into *good* habits. I was set in my ways for sure, but I realized I had been so wrong about other things that maybe I was also wrong in thinking that I couldn't change. I was willing to let go of my pride, to stop and listen. I finally realized that it could only get better. It sure couldn't get any worse.

When you lose the trust of your spouse, children, parents, and friends, reality hits like a hammer, and you feel your life has become a nightmare. In fact, a nightmare might be better than times like these, because nightmares aren't real. A bad reality is infinitely worse than a bad dream.

So, one day the addict in want of recovery

says, "I want to change. What do I do? Where do I go? Is it too late?"

Every person in recovery remembers asking these questions – the exact moment they were ready to change their lives, for once and for all.

The day I came to this decision was full of emotion. I gave my life and my will to Jesus once again, and I meant it this time. That gave me strength, but the next thing I was told brought relief – *it was not too late for me to recover from my addictions and become a woman of God.*

At this point the addict asks, "I realize I am powerless over my addictions, but I want help – now what? What do I do next? Where do I go? What do I do? *Is it really never too late?*"

The answers to these questions are elusive when the desperate addict asks them. It's almost like they are a secret, although after a while it seems that everybody around you knows the answers. That is when you are surrounded by other people in recovery. The veil is lifted, and things that were once so confusing become simple – and the best thing is that *it is never too late*.

It is never too late to become a servant of God. He is the alpha and omega, the beginning and the end, infinite. If you have only one second left, you have plenty of time. Turn your will and your life over to Jesus, and you are saved. *It is never too late.*

I cried for hours that day. Tears of joy and tears of remorse and pain rained from my eyes. I was ready to start a new life, desperate to do so.

A question burned in me – *where do I start?* I had attempted to clean up my life numerous times, starting at the age of twenty-seven, but I had not succeeded. I was formally saved at the age of thirty-two at Faith Family Church in Victoria, Texas. Like many others, I thought that because I was saved I would naturally stop drinking and drugging, because God was going to handle it for me. That was a trap the devil had set. Satan wanted me to forget that earth was his domain, full of temptation. I mistakenly thought that everything would be peaches and cream, if I said certain words.

Like many others, I got the memo, but I didn't understand the message. I had to do my part, too. God was infinitely willing to help me, if I was willing to help myself – and if I was willing to help others.

In my weak, shattered, and vulnerable state, I could never have known that I was going to be on a roller coaster ride for the next thirteen years. Thirteen years seems like so long, but looking back, it seems to have passed in thirteen minutes. My life did not change to what it is today until I completely understood the difference between my will and God's will. It took me thirteen years to figure out that *my* will did not work.

A drunk never wants to give his keys to the designated driver for some reason, even though it would be so much nicer to relinquish control and ride home safely in the passenger seat. That is an apt comparison to those of us who aren't willing to put our life in God's hands when we are severely in danger of hurting ourselves or others. Getting past this type of stubborn thinking is a major hurdle, but also a major accomplishment, when overcome.

I didn't know how to fix the damage I had caused – what was done was done. The reality was that I could not fix things in the past – I could only make amends and ask for forgiveness from those I had harmed. I wondered whether it was too late to change my ways and too late for God to change me. I felt like I had already missed my purpose that He had planned for me – so many years had been wasted. How could He fix the mess that I had gotten myself into? Would I ever be able to give it all to Him? I had question after question.

That day, I realized I had lost any real faith in the Lord that I ever had. It wasn't done on purpose – I had just stopped doing my part in my relationship with God. I needed to start over by having the faith that it was not too late and knowing I could not do it without God. I also realized that I better start remembering why Jesus gave his life for humanity. I was determined to fight for my life – the one Jesus died for.

God showed me a scripture in the Bible that clearly stated to me that "*He did not want me to die; instead He wanted me to show what He did for me.*" **Psalms 118:17**. How amazing is that? I realized that the answers to all those questions I had were in the Bible. I was slowly understanding that God had every answer to every one of my questions, but I had to have faith.

I witnessed God in action one day at Pastor Tamara's weekly Bible study at Faith Family Church. When she asked if anyone needed to pray the Sinner's Prayer or rededicate their life to Jesus, I didn't hesitate – I raised my hand and stood up and said, "I would like to rededicate my life to Jesus." She said the Sinner's Prayer with me, and at that moment the Holy Spirit took away my anxiety. I knew the second I finished saying that prayer that I was forgiven by God through Christ and that I was going to be just fine. It was an amazing, awesome feeling.

Not long after, I locked myself in a small chapel, and I was not leaving until I had a heart-to-heart talk with God. It was just me and Him, and I was more serious about the conversation I was going to have with Him than I ever had been in my entire life. I'll never forget how amazing that day was. I fell to my knees and prayed and cried, then prayed and cried some more, until I felt God reach out to me and help me back to my feet. I looked up and said, "God, I don't want to do my will any more. Look what it has caused in my life – so much guilt and pain. I want to stop hurting others. Please help me live Your purpose and give me strength to carry on and live a life with You."

I felt the presence of God all around that little chapel, and He revealed something to me. I had a vision of books falling off a shelf, one after another. In this vision, the chapel became filled with spirits, more women than men, so I shared and ministered to them about restoration and deliverance through Jesus Christ. I was in the chapel for about three hours, and when I walked out I was on a natural high that came from the Holy Spirit. I felt like I was walking three feet off the ground. You know why? – Jesus carried me out of the chapel. My relationship with God became the most important thing in my life, and I understood that He was able to reconcile both my will and His will. Through Jesus Christ I found my purpose that day – the purpose I thought was too late to get back.

God started guiding changes in my personality, my behaviors, my attitude, how I treated others – everything. He made known His will for me to help others, while serving Him and relying on faith. He showed me how to walk in the spirit and get out of my own flesh. He gave me a genuine desire to change my life. He showed me how to love, trust, and respect myself. I know in my heart that I could not have made changes like these without God. Jesus said, *"With men this is impossible, but with God all things are possible"*. **Matthew 19:26**.

If you are struggling with addictions or other problems, you may feel like something is wrong with you. You are sick and tired of being sick and tired. You may even go to church every Sunday and tell yourself, "I'm going to make the right choices from now on." A week goes by and you are again making the wrong choices. It's the sinful nature that we live in.

Romans 7:18 says, *"And I know that nothing good lives in me, that is, in my sinful nature. I want to do what is right, but I can't. I want to do what is good, but I don't. I don't want to do what is wrong, but I do it anyway. But if I do what I don't want to do, I am not really the one doing wrong; it is sin living in me that does it".*

Making changes in your life can be the hardest or the easiest thing you do for yourself. It all depends on how bad you really want to live an abundant life. So many people miss out on their blessings and the purpose God has for them, because they fear change. One day they'll wish they could get all that time back – the time they wasted by resisting change.

The thought of giving up things in your life that have been such a big part of it for so long may sound scary. Take a long look at your life, your behavior, and your habits. In recovery, it's called taking a personal inventory. Are you happy? Do you have peace in your heart? Do you have a relationship with God? If your answers are no, then it may be time to make some changes. If change scares you, then be like me and *do it afraid*! Just do it – it will be worth it. Fear is one of the primary reasons we stay addicted. God can take that fear away if you have faith in Him.

We need to take action as Esther in the Bible did – she risked her life to save her people from death, simply by trusting God. When she trusted God, He gave her the courage to act at the right time. She could have remained selfishly silent and had her people pay their lives for the disrespectful act that was done by her cousin, Mordecai, but she did the right thing.

My pastor always says, "Show me your friends, and I will show you your future." If you have friends that drink, you will eventually drink. If you are hanging out with friends that do drugs, you will do drugs. But, if you hang out with friends that pray, you will also pray. God will always provide you with new friends. You will never be alone. I have more friends today than I've ever had. It can be the same for you.

When I became faithful to God, I changed my lifestyle. The 'friends' I used to have don't even call or look for me anymore. God will do his part in restoring you, but you have to be willing to change people, places, and things in your life.

It all starts with who you surround yourself with. You might think, "I will never be able to do this. My friends are like my family. I have known them all my life. We drink together and have fun."

But, if your addiction is alcohol, and you are working on sobriety, the smartest thing is to let them know you would appreciate it if they would not drink around you. Let them know you have changed your life and share the good news with them. If they are truly your friends, they will respect your wishes. If they don't respect your sobriety, you need some new friends.

If your friends do drugs, believe me – when they find out you are walking with God and changing your life, they are not going to call you anymore. Be careful, though – Satan will use them to tempt you. You may work with them or run into them at the store. Staying away from users will be a choice you will have to make, and you need to be strong. Letting go of the wrong people in your life will not be easy. It's going to take belief and trust in God. *"All praise to God, the Father of our Lord Jesus Christ, who has blessed us with every spiritual blessing in the heavenly realms because we are united with Christ."* **Ephesians 1:3**.

At this time I want to talk about another thing that can make it very hard to start and maintain recovery – pride. Be it real or false, overcoming pride can be just as important as overcoming fear.

I don't remember as a young girl ever having any dreams or hope to be successful in life. I just knew I wanted to work and have money, so I wouldn't have to live off the government. I came to that opinion from watching my mom. Even though my grandparents provided us a nice home, my mother still worked to help pay bills. She worked hard, but as most single mothers who don't receive child support do, she took some government assistance to help make ends meet. I never wanted to do that, unless absolutely necessary.

I was aware we didn't have much money, and my sisters and I didn't have as much luxury as my cousins. Most of my clothes were made by my mother. I learned what being poor was when I was at the corner store with my sisters, and we all had a dollar food stamp coupon in our hand to pay for our candy. The neighborhood kids were there and started to laugh at us, making fun of us for being on welfare. They teased that we were the poorest kids in the neighborhood. From that day on, I was embarrassed and ashamed. When I got to high school, I refused to take free lunch, so I would go all day without eating. My pride took over and wouldn't let me suffer further embarrassment.

As I got older, I grew to respect my mother so much more. I realized that she did what she had to do, even if it meant being on welfare for a year or two. That government assistance made her able to go to college, so she could provide for her family. I was about twelve years old when my mother graduated from college. It taught me that anything can be accomplished through hard work and sacrifice.

As a child and teenager, I had false pride and wouldn't admit my family was poor. As an adult, my pride kept me from admitting I had an addiction. I would lie through my teeth, rather than confess that I had a drug addiction or that someone had broken my heart. Pride kept me from seeing the ugliness within me, because it kept me from admitting my problems and flaws. **Proverbs 11:2** says, *"Pride leads to disgrace."* Pride can be used as a false front that keeps us from admitting our dark secrets to others and even ourselves.

When I mentioned in Part One about not believing my mother made the right choices in babysitters, I said it for a reason. I will now share some painful memories regarding that subject.

I was molested by one of my babysitter's sons. I was about five years old, and he was probably in his early twenties. As I laid in bed to sleep, he would lay with me and have me touch him inappropriately throughout the night. I also remember being at another babysitter's house where the older boys, probably early teens, would hold me down in bed and lie on top of me while they touched me and kissed me. Adults were in the same room and didn't even stop it.

I remember being so scared, because both these things happened more than once. Each time, I was told if I said anything I would die, so I never shared those painful stories with my mother or anyone else until I was in my forties.

The fear I carried with me throughout my childhood as the result of these experiences gave me a low self-esteem. I was ashamed to talk about it, because I always felt like maybe I did something wrong and deserved the things that happened to me or somehow caused them. I completely blocked these incidents out of my mind as if they had never happened, but I never forgot about them. I had too much pride to talk about it.

I never realized how much this affected my life until I opened up and talked about it to someone. When I was in rehab, one of the first questions I was asked was if I had ever been molested or sexually abused. My first response was, "No I haven't", but I knew I was lying.

I remember God speaking to my heart, saying, "Tell the truth and the truth will set you free." I sat there shaking and crying. In my mind, I was thinking, "Let go and listen to God. Let him help you." I was selfish – my pride, shame, and denial had blocked God from removing my shortcomings and restoring me. I closed my eyes and asked Him to help me accept the truth and deal with the painful memories from childhood. I had denied the feelings my entire life and needed to be set free from the hurt inside. I trusted God and told the truth to my counselor and started to feel relief. I knew I was on the road to recovery.

It's never too late to be set free from any destruction that you may still hold in your heart. You must come to the place of giving up our prideful self-sufficiency. You must also be willing to ask for help. When you depend on God, you will realize He is always there for you, no matter how much shame you carry or what has happened in the past. The freedom you will receive is unbelievable, and you'll wish you had been honest with yourself and God years ago.

Make a decision today to ask God to help you overcome the hurt and pain you carry. Ask Him for the courage to honestly talk to someone about your situation.

In **Luke 11:9-10**, *"Jesus said and so I tell you, keep on asking and you will receive what you ask for. Keep on seeking, and you will find. Keep on knocking and the door will be opened to you. For everyone who asks, receives. Everyone who seeks, finds. And to everyone who knocks, the door will be opened."*

God wants you to learn from what you have been through, so you can help others who are fighting what you once fought. Many of our shortcomings come from our past hurts. Being poor might give you false pride. Being molested might give you bitter resentments and shame. Hate, anger, and low self-esteem can come from any number of things all of us have experienced in life. The recovery process will help you sort out all these feelings, so you can heal yourself and help someone else find healing.

God provides us with many Christian programs that can guide us through our recovery. From the start, it is about letting God work in you and accepting that you are powerless over your addictions. You have to be willing to allow Him to cleanse you from the inside out. You have to get rid of the old pain to bring in the new peace. Jesus couldn't have said it any more perfectly, when he said in **Matthew 9:17**, *"And no one puts new wine into old wineskins. For the new wine would* *burst the skins from the pressure, spilling the wine and ruining the skins. New wine is stored in new wineskins so that both are preserved."*

Understanding that scripture is key to understanding recovery. When you admit that you are powerless and that life has become unmanageable, you will be able to empty yourself of the pain that feeds your addiction, if you are honest. Your earthly vessel will be emptied and ready to re-fill with God and what He wants for your life.

I am sure you have a story like mine, maybe even worse. I used to think I was different than you, but now I know how similar we are. Some of us don't even live to tell their story and find recovery. Pray to God that will not be you. If you are heading in the wrong direction, make a u-turn. Turn your life over to Jesus, let go and let God. And remember – **It's Never Too Late!**

PART FOUR: *SATAN'S STRONGHOLDS*

What are strongholds? Strongholds are areas in our mind and thinking that master and imprison us and keep us from being completely free. This is one of the ways Satan can hold us captive. Strongholds are based on lies and deceptions.

In the Bible, Paul wanted to be mastered by nothing but the will of Jesus Christ. He wrote specifically about strongholds.

"For though we live in the world, we do not wage war as the world does. The weapons we fight with are not the weapons of the world. On contrary, they have divine power to demolish strongholds." **II Corinthians 10:3-4**

The word 'strongholds' may sound powerful, because we can allow them to be strong enough to hold us down. With the help of our savior, Jesus Christ, we can break free of them. Strongholds are never as powerful as God's will. Remember, the devil is a liar, and Jesus Christ has given us authority over Satan's power. God has given us the power to destroy all strongholds that start with a bad or evil thought.

Paul said *"For we are not fighting against flesh and blood enemies, but against evil rulers and authorities of the unseen world, against mighty powers in this dark world, and against evil spirits in the heavenly places."* **Ephesians 6:12**. It is important that we understand the true root of our problem. It's not our family, not our spouse, not our children or our jobs. The devil is the real enemy! Like Paul said, our battle is with demonic spirits, not the people in our lives.

We have all battled some type of stronghold – even when we think we have never been mastered by anything. A stronghold can be an emotion such as jealousy, bitterness, resentment, anger, insecurity, or just having a negative attitude about life. Remember, strongholds are mental issues, not problems with the people around you. They will definitely cause problems with the people in your life, though.

The strongholds I have battled in my life are many. The most predominant one has been pride, which led me to be a liar, boastful of a life I did not really have. Another big one has been my insecurity, which caused me to be shameful. These types of strongholds led me to become a liar, which in turn fed my addictions and selfishness.

Before I found true faith in God, my strongholds controlled my actions. In fact, I was completely unaware of them. I thought I was made to be the person I was and could never change. I didn't like who I was, but I was surrounded by people doing the same bad things as me, so I had no reason to honestly evaluate my inner self. I lived most of my life with the thought that I was not supposed to become anyone other than the person I was at that moment.

It was during the beginning of my walk with God that I realized I needed to get connected with some type of Christian support program. I knew I needed God in my recovery if I was going to overcome addiction. This is when I reached out to Celebrate Recovery. I learned it was a program for overcoming different types of hang-ups – not just drugs or alcohol. I knew I had a lot more going wrong with my life than just an addiction. It was during this time that I had to face my demons (strongholds) face to face.

Fighting your demons is a battle of life and death – *your life or death*. It's one you have to face if you ever want to overcome your problems, just like David, who confronted Goliath. Although just a teenager, David faced his terrifying enemy with confidence. David trusted God, so he could stand up to any intimidation. Like him, you have to believe there is a God who can help you if you ask. Jesus tells us in **Mark 9:23**, *'Jesus said everything is possible for him who believes.'*

In Celebrate Recovery, I learned how to recognize my strongholds. That's the first step we have to take, because usually we don't see inner demons without taking a hard look inward. We have become comfortable with our personality defects and don't even notice the toll they take on our lives. The next step is to take a long look at ourselves and accept responsibility for the hurtful things we have done in our lives. Eventually, you should make amends to those you have harmed.

We must learn to use spiritual weapons. When David conquered Goliath, it had more to do with his spiritual weapons than his sling-shot. When we study the word of God, we learn to use the 'Whole Armor of God'. We are challenged to *"stand firm then, with the belt of truth buckled around your waist, with the breastplate of righteousness in place, and with your feet fitted with the readiness that comes from the gospel of peace. In addition to all this, take up the shield of faith, with which you can extinguish all the flaming arrows of the evil one. Take the helmet of salvation and the sword of the Spirit, which is the word of God."* **Ephesians 6:14-17**

How do we break strongholds? Here are some things I do that keep me strong and give me strength daily.

1. The most important thing is to remember that you are never alone. In **Hebrews 13:5-6**, God said to us, *"I will never fail you, I will never abandon you,"* so we can say, *"The Lord is my helper, so I will have no fear."* God is always with us. He wants you to call on him in your time of

need. You will need Him the most as you battle your strongholds. I can honestly say from experience that it can't be done without Him.

2. We need to have faith and believe that our faith is a powerful weapon against the enemy. In **1 John 5:4** we are reassured, because it says, *"for every child of God defeats this evil world, and we achieve this victory through our faith, and who can win this battle against the world? Only those who believe that Jesus is the Son of God"*.

3. We have to take authority. Every believer has the right to use the authority of Jesus' name to battle Satan's actions. We take authority through our prayer life and our daily Bible reading. The strength of our faith comes from spending quality time with God.

4. We stay connected. We come together with other Christians to pray and intercede against strongholds until we get results. Jesus said in **Matthew 18:19**, *"If two of you agree here on earth concerning anything you ask, my father in heaven will do it for you"*.

5. Submit yourself to God and draw close to Him. Submit to Jesus and know that the Holy Spirit is within you. When you do this, the devil will run from your life with his tail between his legs. Make Jesus Christ your source of strength – it will be the best decision you ever made.

6. Love yourself more than any stronghold. Remember, strongholds are from the devil, and we are from God. God made you the beautiful person you are today. Don't take your dreams to the grave – live them now. Always believe that with God all things are possible and that you are good enough to do his work. It doesn't matter where you've been or what you have done – you have a purpose to fulfill and God has forgiven all of us.

God will help you through any battle you fight to overcome your stronghold, but remember that you have a part to play and your part is very important. It's going to be hard work, but God will help you if you ask him. Open your heart and mind and become obedient and disciplined. Your life will change for the better. And remember – ***It's Never Too Late!***

PART FIVE: *Freedom*

Freedom comes when we celebrate God's love and live a full, joyful life. With that freedom will come a peaceful heart and a peaceful mind. When you have the ability to love yourself and love and serve others, you will be free of bondage and you will realize that with God all things are possible.

Galatians 5:1 *"So Christ has truly set us free. Now make sure that you stay free, and don't get tied up again in slavery..."* The message Paul was sending is that we have to depend on Jesus alone for salvation and daily strength. Do not become a slave to addiction. We must avoid the destructive tendencies of man.

Ezekiel 36:24-27 *"For I will gather you up from all the nations and bring you home again to your land. Then I will sprinkle clean water on you, and you will be clean. Your filth will be washed away, and you will no longer worship idols. And I will give you a new heart, and I will put a new spirit in you. I will take out your stony, stubborn heart and give you a tender responsive heart."* Even though we may not deserve it, God promises to give us a new heart and fill it with His spirit so we can make the right decisions in our lives.

John 8:31-32 *"Jesus said to the people who believed in him, you are truly my disciples if* *you remain faithful to my teachings. And you will know the truth and the truth will set you free."* To be 'set free' is to know the truth – the truth about ourselves and about Jesus Christ. The truth is this: we are in bondage of sin, which makes us become powerless to manage our lives. With God's truth implanted in our hearts, we can recognize and confess our sins. When we turn our broken lives over to God, he can make us whole again.

When you are in slavery or bondage of some kind, God can hear you call out to Him just as He heard the Israelites call out to Him for help when they wandered the desert. Sometimes it may take hitting rock bottom before you can admit you are powerless over your circumstances, but when you turn to God, He will deliver you.

You have to be patient and let God do things His way in His time. What I found during my time of waiting on God was that having patience was very difficult. I knew I trusted Him, though, so I continued to do my part and work on 'my stuff'. I gave up all my control to Him so that I would be set free, slowly but surely. I had to remember that I didn't get messed up over night, and I wasn't going to get fixed over night, either.

I knew God didn't want me to be alone while I was working on myself, so I surrounded myself with others who wanted the same thing as me. Celebrate Recovery was where I found people who wanted to help me find God and deliverance. It took a lot of hard work and time – I was in and out of Celebrate Recovery for seven years before it finally took hold for once and for all. What saved me was including God in my life and working the program, step by step. The key to it all was doing it honestly and faithfully. To work the program was the best decision I ever made, but I couldn't have done it without God. I give all the glory to Him for turning my life around.

I love going to bed feeling safe and worry free, trusting that the next day will be better than the last. I wake up knowing the Holy Spirit is going to direct me and guide me in all I do. I have true faith in God.

Your life doesn't have to be full of destruction. You can live a happy, fulfilled life, free from broken promises. God provides the perfect example, because He keeps all His promises. Remember that God *does* exist, and you *do* matter to him. Most importantly, you have to believe that He has the power to help you recover from whatever the enemy is attacking you with. If you can begin with that planted in your heart, then you are off to a successful recovery.

"God is working in you, giving you the desire and the power to do what pleases Him." **Philippians 2:13**

PART SIX: *Women Rich In Faith*

In 2007, my passion was helping others through the Celebrate Recovery program. I had mastered the program enough to know what I had to do to preserve my sanity. I also knew God wanted me to help other people receive the same understanding. I wanted to share my strength and hope and guide women to God and a recovery program, so they could live a life of joy, peace and love. I wanted other women to know they didn't have to live a life of pride, guilt, and shame.

At that time in my life, I had a nice paying job, but it took a lot of my time. This was early in my time of being a single, sober woman in recovery. Starting my ministry was going to be hard work, but God was feeding my spirit with His word. My work days averaged about ten hours, but sometimes I pulled fourteen hour shifts and didn't get home until two in the morning. My job also required me to work many times on days when I was supposed to be off. I had an agreement with my boss to take breaks from my job to attend church on Wednesday nights and did the same to lead the chemical dependency class for the women at Celebrate Recovery on Thursday nights.

Thankfully, I was off most Mondays, which allowed me to complete my first year of the Destiny Bible Institute at the church. I was able to attend church faithfully on Sunday mornings, as well, and supported or led the Sunday morning Celebrate Recovery class, when needed. My activities at the church took up almost all of my time away from work. I lived life in this manner for almost two years.

In 2009, God led me to start a small Bible study group at my home. I invited women and their children to come over on Sunday evening, and I would cook dinner. We would do a study from the Bible and have fellowship. My heart led me to help women who had distractions or hang-ups that kept them away from their walk with God. I would pick many of them up and then drive them back home after our meeting. I loved every minute of it. I knew it was my calling.

My job was no longer fitting in with the plans God had for me. I knew I had to make some changes if I was going to fulfill the vision I saw back in that little chapel years before. I didn't see myself changing jobs, though. I hoped God would work things out for me, so I could focus on my woman's group, finish my courses at Destiny Bible Institute, and most of all finish this book.

I prayed and fasted and gave the control to God. I believed He was going to accomplish His work through me, and I had faith. I knew He might call on me to make major adjustments to my life.

For over fifteen years, when I needed to get away and ease my mind, I would go into the Goodwill stores. I would browse for hours sometimes. It relaxed me. I enjoyed visiting with the employees and finding interesting items. Never would I have thought the Goodwill store would have been the job God was going to put me in, but it was! It gave me the perfect schedule, and also allowed me to work for a company that was helping people. Goodwill is a nonprofit organization – a respectful business that uses 95 cents of each $1.00 spent there to aid the disabled and put people to work. I love their mission! After three interviews, I was offered the position of store manager. The district manager, Mike Baggio, said he saw something in me when we first met – that not only was I going to run a great business, but he also saw God was working in me. He knew the job was for me.

It was the perfect job, not only to do the things God had planned for me, but also to help others find peace in their hearts. When I learned that a pastor had founded Goodwill in the early 1900's, I knew I belonged there. Today, I manage the successful Goodwill store in Victoria, Texas. I can't count how many lives I've seen changed since I've been there. I love sharing my testimony, especially with those who come in to do community service hours for probation.

Now that I was working less hours, it was time to re-focus my energy on my woman's ministry. I was now going to be able to go back to DBI, plus focus on this book. Being that Goodwill is a non-profit, I had to take a cut in pay compared to my last job. I was going to have to walk by faith, make adjustments, be obedient, and open my heart for a new experience with God. I was advised by several people not to take the job, but I knew it was what God wanted for me.

When I got to Goodwill, I met a young girl named Holly who worked there. She was soft-hearted, sweet, and a beautiful young woman. She shared her past experience with me about how she once served the Lord in her home state of Michigan. She had a heart for God, and I could see it. I invited her to church, and immediately she was back on track in serving the Lord. She became a big part of my life and was a true blessing to me when I was starting my ministry.

Holly has since moved out of town, but she is still serving the Lord. She and I faithfully keep in touch, and I want to share a little something she wrote for me that truly touched my heart.

You are beautiful... your heart is of gold, your passion inspires and your voice is easy. I could sit and listen to you speak forever. It's the way you insist with your eyes on looking directly into the soul of the person who has your attention... your precious attention that you so generously offer. Your intensity is in wonderful tandem with the most beautiful smile that has blessed my life. You're a gift from heaven and your words are always genuine, coming directly from a movement in your heart. You are radiant. His heart is stirred by you... never change that, no one else does it quite as perfectly as you do. You are a servant of the King, and you make Him the proudest of fathers. You're his daughter, you're changing lives, and he is always with you, always smiling because you my friend are great and are a true door to his undying love- Holly

The reason I chose to share what Holly wrote to me is not for personal glorification. I want to illustrate how much you can connect with another person simply by doing God's will and trying to be the best friend you can. If you are doing what God intends, people will see it in you, even if you haven't said a word.

I also met another person about this time – Matt Syverson. I know God directed our meeting. When we first talked, we discovered that we were both writing books. Matt was farther along than me and almost ready to self-publish his book. He was willing to help me through the complicated process, even serving as my editor. The two of us working together has blessed both our lives. I hope we will be friends for life.

It's Never 80 Too Late

Things began to change tremendously and beautifully. Within a month, my bible study became a small group for women at my church, which I named 'Women Rich in Faith Ministry'. The first year was a learning experience. I had some challenges, but I was determined not to give up. Instead, I kept pushing and trusting God. The group started to interest more women – some would come and some would go.

I knew I would eventually have to provide childcare as the group expanded. All along, God had provided me with the tools to fulfill His purpose, so I trusted He would help me when the time came, and He did.

I will share a story with you that illustrates how God provides and prepares us for his purpose. When I was in rehab, my counselor encouraged me to pick up a hobby. One hobby available to me was an opportunity to learn how to make jewelry. I honestly didn't want to do it – all I wanted to do was get my life together and go home. I remember having a bad attitude at one point about it. Then, the Holy Spirit reminded me that I was there to learn obedience. I decided to make the best of it and learned how to make jewelry. Little did I know, it was a God-sent moment. Today, my jewelry sales support the needs of my ministry and also paid all the expenses to publish this book. Tell me that isn't God working....

It's Never 81 Too Late

I enrolled back into DBI. I was leading the Chemical Dependency group for the women at Celebrate Recovery, as well as teaching the principles of Celebrate Recovery at the juvenile detention center.

I was doing so much that I needed to pull back a little and focus more on Women Rich In Faith. I remember praying about it, and all I could see was the vision that God had shown me in the little chapel. So, I put my focus into DBI, Women Rich in Faith, and this book, and reminded myself that the things I wanted to accomplish would come in God's timing.

I graduated from the Destiny Bible Institute in June of 2011. I've since decided to continue my education and take another year in a master's program. I am eager to learn more about God's word, which will keep the Holy Spirit burning in me.

I would like to share a story about a friend of mine named Fred. About a year before the publication of this book, Fred came in to the Celebrate Recovery program very broken. He was going through a divorce and was basically mourning the loss of his loved one, although she was not dead. I remembered Fred from high school and immediately befriended him.

One night, Fred wanted to give up – he

walked out of the Celebrate Recovery meeting crying. I ran after him and stopped him before he got in his car. I said, "Fred, please don't go! I know exactly how you are feeling, because I went through the same thing. If God got me through it, He will get you through it, too!"

I grabbed his hand and said, "Come on, let's go back inside." He looked at me and smiled. We walked back into the meeting together. Fred continued to attend Celebrate Recovery. He became a leader and started helping others. Over the course of the next year, Fred and I became close friends. On July 8, 2011, as I was traveling to go set up for a Women Rich In Faith event, my phone rang. Normally, I try not to answer my phone when I am driving, but when I looked across the seat, I saw that it was Fred. I almost didn't answer, but I felt the Holy Spirit telling me to do so.

I answered the phone. Fred said that he was just calling to say hello. He thanked me for not letting him leave Celebrate Recovery that night when he was so upset. He told me he thought the world of me, and I assured him I felt the same about him. He mentioned how happy he was to be working with the prison ministry. He told me he was happy and full of joy before he hung up.

I felt so much warmth for him. I was so pleased that I had been able to help Fred turn his life around. That evening, I continued with my plans, and we had a great Women Rich In Faith meeting. A few hours after that call, Fred went to be with the Lord unexpectedly. From what he told me earlier, I know he died happy.

I know Fred is in heaven now, which brings me peace. The awesome thing about my relationship with Fred isn't just his success at overcoming the pain at the loss of his wife. It's that he helped keep me sober. That's the way recovery works. Helping other people is what ends up keeping *you* sober. I'm so blessed to have known Fred.

As I continue to walk my path with Jesus, not only do I live life with a peaceful soul, but my daddy is also serving the Lord faithfully. He has also been set free from his hangups and has been sober for almost twenty years. My relationship with my mother is absolutely wonderful, and she is still happily married to my step-dad, Steve.

As for my daughters, I thank God for them everyday. Brandi met a wonderful man, Daniel, and they are happily married. He serves in the Air Force, and is stationed in Minot, North Dakota. Seth now has a new sister, Mckenzie Faith, and a dad he loves very much. As for Sara, she serves the Lord right beside me as the assistant director of the Women Rich in Faith Ministry. She plans to continue to help me build the ministry.

It's Never 84 Too Late

The relationship I have with both my daughters is the best gift that I hold to my heart from God. I treasure every moment that I spend with them. I enjoy every one of Landon's football games and watching Nathan and Kaylie as they start their first year in school. I enjoy the visits with Seth and Mckenzie and love watching them grow up to be future servants of God. The time that I lost in my life is now a memory, replaced with joy and laughter and priceless moments. Only God could have made this possible in my life today.

Women Rich In Faith has evolved over the last two years. We now meet the second and fourth Friday evenings of each month. At each meeting we worship, have fellowship, and listen to a speaker. Now, more than ever, the mission is to help women find God and personal recovery. It is important to note that Women Rich In Faith is a support group now, not a Bible study. *"We are women who believe that our faith in Jesus has set us free... and free we are!"*

Women Rich In Faith remains dedicated to helping women find what I once wished for – to live happy, joyous, and free. Our mission is to help and encourage women to find the one true love – Jesus Christ – and to know that they are never alone. The women attending the ministry come from varied backgrounds. Some attend because they are hurting from a relationship. Some have been abused. Some are codependent. Some are battling addiction, and some are just coming to connect with other women and see old friends. Whatever the reason for getting there, all Women Rich In Faith are equal, and all are welcome!

Another blessing in the ministry is that we have ladies ranging in age from twelve to over sixty. I learned years ago that age is just a number, and that the old and young both have something to teach the other.

As I write this book, I don't know where God is taking this ministry, but I do know that it is His ministry, and it has been fruitful for many. I've seen women walk through our doors and find serenity. It gives ladies a place where they can feel welcome and supported. I've seen women come in who didn't even believe in God, but now serve Him faithfully. This ministry is changing lives for the better.

Women Rich In Faith is still young, but God has a plan for it. The women and I will continue to faithfully carry God's message and offer help wherever possible. We will continue to travel to retreats, rehabs, nursing homes, woman's shelters, and outreaches to do whatever we can to spread the word of God.

For God is the only true way to a complete

restoration. *"Your word is the lamp to my feet and a light for my path."* **Psalms 119:105.** When you put God first in your life, everything else will fall into place. Paul gives us a word of encouragement in **Philippians 4:6-7**, *"Don't worry about anything: instead, pray about everything. Tell God what you need, and thank Him for all He has done. Then you will experience God's peace, which exceeds anything we can understand. His peace will guard your hearts and minds as you live in Christ Jesus."*

"Let the message about Christ, in all its richness, fill your lives. Teach and counsel each other with all the wisdom He gives. Sing psalms and hymns and spiritual songs to God with a thankful heart. And whatever you do or say do it as a representative of the Lord Jesus, giving thanks through Him to God the father". **Colossians 3:16-17**

"Now all Glory to God, who is able, through His mighty power at work within us, to accomplish infinitely more than we might ask or think." **Ephesians 3:20**

Just remember – no matter what you been through or what you have done, *it is never too late* to make a life changing choice.

GOD BLESS YOU!

It's Never 87 Too Late

www.ingramcontent.com/pod-product-compliance
Lightning Source LLC
Chambersburg PA
CBHW031412040426
42444CB00005B/531